MATERFAMILIAS

BY

KIMBERLY GLADMAN JACKSON

Copyright © 2018 Kimberly Gladman Jackson

All rights reserved. This book or any portion thereof may not be reproduced or used in any manner whatsoever without the express written permission of the publisher except for the use of brief quotations in a book review.

Printed in the United States of America

First Printing 2018

ISBN-13: 978-0-9998455-0-9

Tandeta Books
1601 Centre St.
Newton, MA 02461

For Sofia and Samuel
someday

Contents

How to Read This Book	1
Swimming with Dolphins	3
Materfamilias	5
Fantasy Donations in Memory of Kayla Mueller	6
Rosary	8
What the Psalmist Knew	11
Mother and Child	12
Yes I	13
Menopausal	15
Saturday 9:35:05 AM	17
Noli Me Tangere	18
On Wandering	20
The Soliloquy of Ginny	21
Entanglement	24
Tonglen for Rin Norris	27
Candle-lighting	28
C-NSOR-D	30
Kevin Knows Color	32
Resurrection	35
The Bride Stripped Bare	36
Saving Grace	39
The Glassine Lizard	41
The Shape-Shifters' Guide To US Travel	42
Site-Specific	46
Anatomy Scan	48
Hannah	49
Ghost Crowd at the Visitors' Center	50
Credo	53
Living Water	55
Week of Wonders	57
Acknowledgements	59

How to Read This Book

This book is a collection of poems in which each piece is accompanied by an author's note that tells you a little something about how and why it was written. (This is a form of author's note I began to love when I saw it in the poetry journal *Rattle*.) The notes can be read as mini-stories in themselves, or skipped.

> "Swimming with Dolphins" was written at a time when I was just discovering the power of poetry to help me cope with some very painful life challenges. I had set myself the goal of writing one poem a month, and every time I met the goal, I felt a sense of accomplishment and solace. At one very difficult time, I missed a couple of months, and my friend Rick reminded me to try to start again.

Swimming with Dolphins
for Rick Bennett

Dolphin therapy has been shown to help children and adults with severe physical and mental challenges, sometimes bringing almost miraculous change to situations that had seemed beyond hope.

--Website, Island Dolphin Retreat Center

If I went down to the ocean
could I dive with you
palms on springy-strong blue flank
to the sandy graylit bottom
and then arc up to the sun
turn corkscrews in the spray
to heal my heart?

Can human pain dissolve
in a pod a thousand strong
full of lovemaking and fighting
and a crowd of half-brain dreams
Wish/bliss/nightmare switching on and off till dawn?

Perhaps I'd need to travel
for long hours in your wake
till I learned to see by hearing
and could listen to the coast
Fractal beauty charting sandbars, rocks, and shoals

Maybe your language has a word
for solace floating, safe-unmoored
Or anguish piercing-leaching-vanished in the waves

Or would the silence between whistles
send a message to my soul?

Would I finally see the pattern
that can make what's broken whole
in those lacunae filled with sealight
dappled green and gold?

> "Materfamilias" was written at a time when both my father-in-law and an aunt of my husband's were dying, and I had two small children and a full-time job. I felt both overwhelmed and privileged to be at the center of a struggling, loving family. To write it, I used the luc bat, a Vietnamese poetic form with an intricate rhyme scheme and alternating lines of six and eight syllables.

Materfamilias

She is both warp and weft;
When fibers fray, she deftly weaves
Them whole. At times, she grieves
Lost freedom, and fears she's less than
Kind. Still, her care joins man,
Child, elders; through her hands run ties
To church, state, world. She lives
In the jeweled net the wise ones teach
Of: facets shine as each
Reflects all others. Reaching far
And deep, her arms and heart
Ache with love—tender, weary, blessed.

> *I wrote the following after reading about Kayla Mueller, a 26-year-old American woman who died in 2015 while being held by the terror group ISIS, and after being repeatedly raped by its leader. Several teenaged Yazidi girls who had been held with her, but managed to escape, reported that they asked her to come with them when they fled. Kayla chose to stay behind, telling them she knew that as an American she was much too conspicuous, and they would have a far better chance of reaching safety without her.*

Fantasy Donations in Memory of Kayla Mueller

Show me where to click
to send guns to the *peshmerga*
To equip its female fighters
with gas masks and hand grenades
With rocket launchers, armored trucks, and bombs
And send me videos of the dead they leave behind

Tell me how many rapists
each $10 can kill
and send me updates on the body count each night
It will soothe my dreams.

Show me where to send my money
to buy out the slave auction
through the undercover agent we will send

to laugh and brag and outbid all the others
and then lead them out the door and set them free

Let me build the camp
where we train good Arab men
to infiltrate and sabotage their plans
so that their armies flee the battle and go home

And let me fund the radio
that softly, close to dawn
plays the lullabies their mothers used to sing
so long ago when they were little boys
who still
loved women

Show me where to click
because my breasts bowels throat are burning
and I see her every time I close my eyes

Show me
Show me
Show me

> "Rosary" was written immediately after the mass killing of schoolchildren in Newtown, Connecticut, in December 2012. In thinking about the grief of those children's mothers, it occurred to me that the central story of Christianity is of a mother grieving her murdered child, and finding a way to live on.

Rosary

Hail Mary
Full of grace
Blessed are you among women
And blessed is the fruit of your womb, Jesus

The baby had colic and money was tight
She was not always patient.
Sometimes at night she wept
Watching his finally—sleeping face
Stroking the tiny foot that would one day be a man's
Fearing what hurt she'd done him in her pain

Holy Mary
Mother of God
Pray for us sinners
Now and at the hour of our death

You get the child you get, not the one you're ready for
When his passion overwhelms him

MATERFAMILIAS

She tries to keep him safe
But she can't understand the things he sees
Sometimes she feels so tired, wants an ordinary boy
But she leads him home and listens to his tales

Hail Mary
Full of grief
Blessed are you among women
And blessed is the fruit of your womb

She saw her child murdered
Held his broken body in her arms.
They make her look young in those pictures
But she was fifty then
And aged at least a decade overnight.
And she did not feel forgiving.

Holy Mary
Mother of God
Pray for us sinners
Now and at the hour of our death.

All the rest came later, after she herself had died
Rock and tomb, signs and tongues, all were comforts
that she had to live without.
Her days broke into moments
always now and now and now:
Give that bread, hold that hand, wipe that brow

Though you don't know if it matters
or makes any sense at all
Do this, he said, do this in memory of me

Holy Mary
Blessed are you
Pray for us

For this is all we have
A touch, a kiss, a word
To fill this fleeting interval of light.

> "What the Psalmist Knew" uses the golden shovel poetic form, which was invented by contemporary poet Terrance Hayes with his poem of that name. In this form, the last words of each line, read in order, form a line from an existing poem (Hayes's poem is an homage to "We Real Cool" by Gwendolyn Brooks). I used it here to express what I feel when I read one of my favorite lines of Scripture, Psalms 98:8.

What the Psalmist Knew
After 98:8

The summer wind is warm for you. Let
it cradle you, and rock. And when the
autumn's earthtilt goldens light, and rivers
chill, hear solace crackling in brown leaves. Through clap
of thunder, grip of ice, know you rest in hands
of earth and sky. Beneath the
naked mud, or snow, or drought-land, hills
ache with hidden green. Make a leap
of faith: drink in the sunrise, for
all revolves, and pain is no truer than joy

> "Mother and Child" is a somonka, a poem made up of two separate poems in the tanka form. Traditionally in Japan, it was written collaboratively by a pair of lovers, with the first part being a declaration of love and the second a response. I adapted it to the maternal relationship.

Mother and Child

You are an organ
Of my body, yet fly free
On thin wings. Who knows
How my words touch deeds will shape
What will soon have been your youth?

Though I can't recall
The day we met, your heart beats
Always in my ears.
Will its solace echo still
If I soar beyond the moon?

> "Yes I" was written in a period when I regularly attended poetry slams at the Nuyorican Poet's Café. I gained an appreciation of rap poetry from listening to the young rappers who would perform for each other while waiting in line to get in, hours before the doors opened. One theme of their work that resonated for me was the quest to be true to oneself and one's authentic experience, however painful it is. Somehow, their themes and their rhythms inspired me to write this piece.

Yes I

In honor of the Nuyorican sidewalk poets
And in memory of Samuel Beckett

I hold myself in arms so still
The silence drills my bones and chills
Me till I know I never will
Know heat—no heat

Cold sweat like pearls upon my skin
With blood like liquid nitrogen
I float beyond all virtue, sin
Or pain—no pain

No judge no jury in this place
I only see the mirror's face
No trace of shame a barren grace

Rains down—rains down

I bear witness to my breath
The flickering flame of life and death
For I will never leave myself
Alone—alone

Sleep now sleep now I say and mean
That even in the darkest dream
A voice survives to wake and scream
I am—I am

I hold myself I'm in my arms
No hope of joy no fear of harm
With nothing left to do or tell
I'm in my arms I hold myself

Without tenderness, but faithfully
Without tenderness, but faithfully
Without tenderness

In faith

> When my doctor told me those times I was waking up sweaty at night were hot flashes and I was menopausal, I felt annoyed at how many negative associations I had to the word. It reminded me of Gloria Steinem's famous essay, "If Men Could Menstruate," in which she imagines feeling proud, instead of embarrassed, about what women's bodies do. I decided it was time to redefine "menopausal" for myself.

Menopausal
A definition in ten flashes

1. *Aporetic*; that is, inclined to doubt or raise objections. From a Platonic dialogue, the Meno, in which Socrates pauses frequently to ask his listeners questions about what virtue is. They don't come up with an answer, but they figure out that a whole lot of bullshit they've heard their whole lives is not true.

2. Vocally and intensely opposed to widely tolerated forms of injustice, especially those affecting women. As in, "I don't know why she said that was sexist. She must be menopausal."

3. Able to view men as potentially delightful sexual partners to whom, however, one has no obligation, and who need not occupy the forefront of one's consciousness. As in, "Men? Oh." (*Pause*)

4. Engaged in an existence-altering transformation of priorities (colloquially termed "change of life") in which one's spiritual, creative, and physical needs are suddenly and vigorously asserted, especially in the face of attempts to deny them. As in, "Get me out of this crowd,I am taking this off *goddamnit* I need some air."

5. Wakeful, at unexpected moments. Burning, from crown to bowels, but still. Lucidly dreaming, with purpose and plan. As in, "Maiden was good, mother was better, and that crone thing: hell yeah, bring it on."

#6-10:

Hot.
Hot.
Hot.
Hot.
Hot.

> "Saturday 9:35:05 AM" was inspired by one of those tiny moments of micro-flirtation that I think gives spice to life, no matter how happily married or how old we are.

Saturday 9:35:05 AM

"It's been so nice talking with you," said the father with the bandana at the pool, "you have a great day," and as I looked back from my kids we slipped the timeline and I dove into his eyes. Into a green space, emerald-shining, soft as down, and feathers everywhere. Sneeze-laughter. His crows' feet turned out to be warm valleys where we rolled down, down, coming to rest, feeling the live earth-flesh breathe beneath our backs. Spooned together like custard, creamy-sweet, we drowsed. Woke to voices of new-familiar children, not his or mine but ours. Watched them play at lakeside, mountains of lush pine beyond. Drank the blue air. Knew that never would there be a cell phone tower there. His hands pillowed my hips, our heartthroatbellies entwined, beating. His millions of cell membranes shimmered, iridescent coral lapis gold, pulsing out a signal. I am here, I am here, though you don't see me, I will always hold you. "You too," I said.

> "Noli Me Tangere" means "touch me not" in Latin, and according to the Gospel of John, is the first thing Jesus said to Mary Magdalene upon emerging from the tomb. The poem was inspired by reading G.K. Chesterton's book about St. Francis, in which he draws attention to this cryptic piece of Scripture. To write it, I used an ancient Celtic poetic form, the rannaicheacht ghairid.

Noli Me Tangere
After John 20:17

Touch me not:
Spirit flows through bone and rock
But I have not ascended
Nor returned to earth flesh blood

So in birth
Mothers' selves swell near to death
Their vibrant terror's lonely
Unseen heart-pulse fills each breath

My hands burn
As skin, soles, breast ache to learn:
Wound is seed; one is many
Pain-bliss sears; sun roars; wind yields.

Speak my name
And taste the desert freedom

MATERFAMILIAS

As ends turn to beginnings
And trees flourish in the flame

> "On Wandering" was written after reading an article about the continuing discrimination against the Romani in Europe, and thinking about why and how we develop a sense of belonging to nations and ethnic groups.

On Wandering

Most of us long, ache, search, for home
Next year, we say, in Jerusalem
Free Kurdistan, Tibet
And who's to say we're wrong?
It makes such simple sense

But the Romani yearn for freedom
No diaspora, they
Are not to be ingathered
When they settle, it's in grief

What they teach is that what matters
Is not where you and yours are from
What forms you is your poetry
Your music, dance, and song

How they terrify the powerful
The makers of passports and maps

> "The Soliloquoy of Ginny" was written after visiting the Providence Zoo and seeing three female elephants who were rescued and brought out of Africa together after poachers killed many of their relatives. One of them rocked continually, in a way that reminded me of a similar behavior by traumatized children. The experience made me wonder whether elephants perhaps have thoughts whose content is similar to ours, but whose grammar is different, and which, of course, cannot be expressed in speech.

The Soliloquy of Ginny, Dominant Elephant at the Providence Zoo, Transmitted Telepathically to the Spectators at her Bath

Katy
colorjoys
here winterdark she brights it
berryred melonpeach grape
trunkbrush sweepsplash
seeglass look

Alice
everrocks   *everrocks*
mother   *poacher*
fathervoice   *silentnow*
rumbleheld   *babygirl*   *free*

Kimberly Gladman Jackson

I
watchlistenthinkfeel
you you you you you you you
painflash laughspark angry crysmile
young young young young young

no milkbreast we

washers   warm
willgood   canweak

by moon
sleep undream
cinderstraw   emptysmell
moon and moon and moon

breathelight morning
remember grass
remember sun
remember river forest plain
know
some still roam

see their eyes clear
hear them trumpet
feel the earth shake as they move
joying evermoon

MATERFAMILIAS

if
you you you you you
breathewith
me

> *I believe that science, psychology, and spirituality are parallel ways of exploring reality, and will ultimately be shown to complement one another. With "Entanglement," I explored the idea that what physicists tell us is true on a microscopic scale might also be operating on the level of our lived experience.*

Entanglement

Entangled particles act as if they are one, even when widely separated: anything that affects one instantaneously affects the other in exactly the same way. Physicists say it happens all the time. A particle of you, right now, could be entangled with a particle of someone you just passed in the street.

Invisibilia Radio Show

The young woman on the train beside me laughs every so often at something she sees on her smartphone. A quiet laugh, but not private: breathy, and really tickled—brimming with something to share. I want to ask *What is it?* Wish her face would turn, and open, and she'd say. But the tablet balanced on her tawny knee informs her of the Cold War's dates (1945-89), while I, shivering in the AC, remember changing dollars for black-market *Ostmarks* outside the Pergamon. As the skyline grows I wonder: does it swell inside her as it does in me, every time, even now? She laughs that

laugh again, and I want to tell her: *Someday the person you're going to marry will think my god, I love the way she laughs. Someday your children's faces will light up when they hear it—it will make them feel that everything's all right.* But of course I can't, and don't, and at the station she is lost beneath the clocks.
****

Crowdflow down Fifth Avenue in January wind. Cartier's, Tiffany's, then her body's dark diagonal. Half-wrapped in a shawl, she rocks. Mutters. Bare head/thin shirt/paper cup/so few coins. The stream of coats legs boots arcs, makes a space. I step in. Place a bill. She sees a 5. *Are you sure?* she says. *You might need this money for something.* When I kneel, her hand is leathery. *God is with you,* I say, though I never believed in him much. She laughs: *That's all I've got left. What's your name?* I tell her. Ask for hers. She tells me, but then the muttering returns. I watch it rock her, draw her in, as the evening snow falls down in searing sheets. When I see a cab, I take it.
****

The slam is starting soon and somebody's taking way too long in the bathroom. The line fidgets. Finally she emerges—halting, then swift—a bare white face with wide eyes almost lashless, a rush of long skirt down the stairs. Later, behind the mike, she reads from a page, her voice clear but just at the threshold of sound. Her words fall, oblique and pearlescent, roll and tumble across the wooden stage until it's covered with a sheen like the inside of skin. The applause is a puzzled sine wave, but one skinny guy in the back is on his feet hollering, and I shout for her too, praying that the current of our gratitude can reach her, and wondering what it is her long sleeves cover.

****

In bed, I watch my belly rise and fall. Somewhere, too, their bodies lie or stretch, in pain or joy or longing I can't know. But as my cells dissolve to molecules and my atoms to their quarks, I feel the pull of what is *mine* and *theirs* in one. The darkness widens, curves through spacetime. Together in our separate orbits, we spin.

> *The following poem was written after reading about Rin Norris, a woman who lost her father and all three of her children—aged 8, 10, and 12—when Malaysian Air Flight 17 was shot down over Ukraine on July 17th, 2014. Tonglen is a Buddhist meditation practice in which one imagines drawing external pain into oneself and in return, sending out compassion and love.*

Tonglen for Rin Norris

Breathing in, I see your boys jostling, peering out the window
Breathing out, I wrap my heart around your ruptured heart

Breathing in, I see your girl draw purple doodles in her notebook
Breathing out, I send starlight through your jagged, hollowed core

Breathing in, I see your father smile as he sips his coffee
Breathing out, I pulse to warm the frozen, shattered channels of your bones

It can't be done. I know.
Home is nowhere, now, nowhere
As slick smoke blackens the midsummer air

> *In the summer of 2014, at least 500 Gazan children were killed by the Israeli military. In the middle of the conflict, Israeli human rights group B'TSelem wanted to read some of the victims' names on the radio, but was banned from doing so by authorities, who said it would be "politically controversial." As I lit Jewish Sabbath candles with my own children, I held these others in mind.*

Candle-lighting

For Joujou, who was sleeping
For Amil, who wanted breakfast
For Suha, who held a stuffed dog
For Ranim and Hana, who held hands

For Walid, who loved seashells
For Aisha, who could run
For Mohammad, who built great forts
For Fatima, who could sing

For Kadeem, whose tooth was wiggly
For Mahmoud, whose tummy ached
For Bassim, who missed his grandma
For Yousef, who had bad dreams

And for all the many others
Twenty-five Newtowns, if not more
Let a sea of light surround them

MATERFAMILIAS

Light a flame
Breathe a prayer
Bless their names

> C-NSOR-D is a poem written without the letter "e," the most commonly-used letter in English. It is written in blank verse (unrhymed iambic pentameter). It came out of my thinking about the many different kinds of censorship and self-censorship that are experienced—and overcome— not only by political activists, but by people experiencing domestic abuse, or those who are oppressed for their sexual orientation or gender identity.

C-NSOR-D

A manuscript in ribbons. Curls of ash
Arising from a plaza full of books.
But also: things a journalist won't say
In print. Unbroadcast facts; illicit songs
Unsung. A woman's body, hiding wounds
From sight; a child's mouth, shut tight against
A truth; a man's half-conscious longing for
A touch that is taboo. And your own thoughts
At night, in visions turbid, aching, dark.
From prison camps to living rooms, in jails
And in our minds—it has a thousand ways
To twist our souls. Now, most of us do try
To fight it. Though it's difficult, you know:
With *samizdat* and cryptograms, our thoughts
Can slip through chains—can fly to mountaintops–
Hang on till *glasnost* finally brings a thaw.
But many bright lights languish and go out

MATERFAMILIAS

For might, not right, may triumph with a blow
Or our own valor stay in short supply
Or any of a million vital links
Fray, just as crisis looms. Support's a must–
For spirits that could soar, if not struck dumb,
May flail in isolation, and succumb.

> As I was working on this book, I was diagnosed with an HER2+ form of breast cancer. My prognosis is relatively good: 85% of people who undergo the treatment I'm now in the middle of are still alive after ten years. But the possibility of being in the other 15%, along with the news that I have the CHEK2 genetic mutation, which raises the odds that I'll get another cancer, has changed my sense of priorities. It seems urgent to me now to live every day as meaningfully and joyfully as I can. And as I strive to do so, I'm amazed at the spiritual gifts I've received from many, many people. Kevin was one of the first.

Kevin Knows Color
For Kevin Thurston

Chemo
Will almost certainly take
The twelve-years' growth I love to feel
Flowing past my shoulders, almost to my waist
The tresses that are as much a part of who I am
As an organ, or a limb.

Before that happens, I want to make a choice.

I don't know your personality he says
But you're having surgery in October
It's breast cancer awareness month
So while we're going short

MATERFAMILIAS

Want to go—pink?

He opens the salon in the evening
And we make it a party
With friends and kids, my husband, his mom
The rabbi, her baby in tow
We say a blessing, drink some wine
and watch him work.

Under his hands, it feels safe
Each snip of the scissors not a loss
But a step on a journey
A movement toward something new.

In the end, when I look up and see
My face framed by his fingers
As he arranges a tendril or two
I think: she is *hot*
She looks like she has *chutzpah*
And my children just laugh and laugh.

He says to come back Thursday
Because he's a crazy colorist
And wants to pink it up even more
But I find his madness divine

I feel like Sarah
Giving birth when she thought it was impossible

Laughing with her midwives
Beneath a desert sky.

> "Resurrection" was written at a moment of personal pain that felt like a kind of death, a moment with no way forward. I was inspired by the story of Lazarus, wrapped in his burial cloths, and yet rising to new life.

Resurrection

To begin again, she'll have to crack the scab's dark wax
And dive, miniaturized, into the swiftly opening fjord

She'll have to hear the currents in the cerebellum folds
Resting warm within the opened bone

Often she'll stand blinking at the empty window
Molecules slipstreaming past their docks

As wind cells travel through her hollows to the poles
Plum-cherry pulse will slowly sweeten flesh

And just beneath the desiccated linen
Thick microbes' pili lead the way to life

> "The Bride Stripped Bare" was written in a week in which, by chance, I had read within a few days of each other some poems by Denise Duhamel, who writes in wonderfully funny and smart ways about sex and gender and women's experience, and an article about the French artist Marcel Duchamp. Somehow, the combination of the themes in both of their work, the repetition of the first syllable in both of their names, and my own associations combined to create this poem.

The Bride Stripped Bare
After Duchamp and Duhamel

Who walks naked down a staircase?
I mean, unless there was a fire in a hotel—
and even then, I'd grab a sheet.
But then, I guess, the stroboscope
just wouldn't look as cool
and no-one wants to watch stop-motion
of a *Man in Business Suit.*
I get it. Still, if lead wire glued to glass
makes you think of sex and pain
it's a sign, if you ask me, that you're obsessed—
and Marcel's problem seemed widespread
among the greats.

MATERFAMILIAS

What made it such a downer
was that I really liked these guys
and I couldn't help but take it personally:
funny subversive Buñuel slicing open a woman's eye
(OK, I know it was a cow, a different kind of *she*)
and brilliant Giacometti
with his thumb-pressed skeletons
haunting empty plazas, and then this:
Woman with her Throat Cut
my pelvis lying there in slaughtered bronze.

I saw my college film prof's point
She saw the *male gaze* like a gun
And I suspected it in every man I knew—
even my husband, who was raised by his grandmother
and became a nurse
and had so many colorful clothes
there was an orange and a purple load
every time we did the wash.

Until one morning, in the half-light
He ran his hands along my curves
And to my murmur-protest *tired* he replied:
You're my experience of beauty
What I find here and here and here
Gives me strength to face the universe each day

It's what makes straight life so confusing:
that we crash together seeking
not just power, but meaning
and feeling not just lust, but love

> *"Saving Grace" was written after a week in which—while both squabbling with and making love to my husband—I had read about how scientists have researched the interior layers of the earth, extrapolating from waves that pass through it what it is made of. I had also been thinking that I wanted to write a poem in a single sentence. These ideas combined to produce this poem.*

Saving Grace

Under the mantle
of worry
bills and fights
far below
the dry plates
of schedule
and snipe
there is a molten core:
slick
and
igneous
pulsing
with sudden laughs
flush of skin
pull of magnet
that steers the poles,
although its
silent force

is only known–
act of reason,
act of faith—
from the shape
of waves
that ripple
through the crust
of doubt

> "The Glassine Lizard" came to me after coming eye to eye with an animal called that in a zoo. It made me think about the elements of consciousness and emotion that may be shared across very different species and situations, including the sensation of confinement and an intense striving against it.

The Glassine Lizard

My God that's an active snake she says. *It's no snake* he says. *Don't bang on the glass* she tells the boys as it rears against the pane, green belly pressing hard. *It's a lizard without legs* he says. Together they read the card: *you can tell them from their eyelids and earslits* he says. *Jake I asked you not to bang on that* she says. *If a predator bites off the tail it can tear free and live* he says. Her black heels shift on the tile. Its head strains up, and up. She meets its pale flat eye. She can see its marrow bubbling: white lava inside the vertebrae. *It's time to go* she says. Her thumb turns the coiled gold, metal on flesh.

> *The following poem was written, and read at the Nuyorican Poet's Café, in December 2014, days after a Staten Island grand jury declined to indict the police officers involved in the choking death of Eric Garner. Garner's daughter, Erica, who became an activist against police brutality, died of asthma-related causes in 2017.*

The Shape-Shifters' Guide To US Travel
In memory of Eric & Erica Garner

Alien visitors to Earth must assume human shape to explore the planet. But those entering the United States of America are urged to use extreme caution when choosing a body vehicle.

The most important rule is to choose one whose external casing has as little pigmentation as possible. Other features of the body will affect how you are treated, including its size and its role in human reproduction. But the protective value of a lack of coloration cannot be overstated.

Under no circumstances should you assume the shape of a large, dark, male.

It is true that our early explorers preferred these shapes, finding them beautiful and strong. But we have lost some of our finest minds in this way, because these shapes are widely hunted.

It is also highly inadvisable to assume the shape of a small dark male. This is because the aggressive light-colored life-forms of this region do not distinguish among dark males, seeing them all as prey.

If, through some error, you find yourself embodied as a dark male, never hold anything in your hands. It was previously believed that dark male embodiment could be practiced safely if the traveler did not carry weapons, but this has been conclusively disproven. We have lost brilliant, intrepid colleagues—spirits who would have charted whole new worlds—due to the handling of wallets and Earthling sweets.

In fact, while in dark male form, it is best not to move your hands or body at all. It was once thought that gestures universally signifying surrender among *homo sapiens* were permissible, but this has also been tragically disproved.

Moreover, speech is counter-indicated while in dark male form, since even non-threatening use of the vocal organs may be met with lethal force.

Do not disregard this advisory in the belief that the recent appointment of a dark male leader has obviated its necessity. Otherwise, you may be the next who dies and whom he mourns, saying, "that could have been me."

Do not ignore this warning in the hope that technology has rendered it obsolete. Or your murder will fly next across the airwaves, its incontrovertible evidence deemed insufficient under the law.

Take heed of this directive before your journey starts. Or we will weep across the galaxies, cursing all the stars in heaven because you're never coming home.

> *This poem-without-title was based on a real experience of finding, during a years-later cleanout of a desk, this record of a hoped-for child who was never born.*

ultrasound photo
in a sealed envelope
back of the drawer

> *In June 2017, the longtime crossing guard at my children's school retired. The occasion made me think about her life's work.*

Site-Specific
For Maureen Cahoon

We are travelers, wanderers, strivers. We struggle.
So we can't help but wonder: what would it be like?
To stand in one spot—or just a few—for a lifetime
To trace a radius around a school
as if with an old-fashioned compass
To be a like a slightly-mobile tree, spreading your arms
for others. To shepherd them with your body,
your voice, your face; to see them safely there
and safely home. For forty-one years, and change

Because so many changes come, and never stop.
And what with budget cuts and squeezes, freezes
I worry that one day they won't replace her
they'll say a traffic light could do as well
some better signage, maybe, if we need it
and come on, can't parents help them cross the street?
But that leaves out her smile
her raised eyebrow, when it's needed
her *how are you* and the way she sees what's funny
Her question: *isn't it a nice day?*
Just rhetorical, but it really makes you think.

MATERFAMILIAS

We need that, see, because even where we are
Our days don't always feel the very best
In fact, beneath it all, some days feel rotten
And it helps, you know, to see the other side.
To think *nonsense, today's bad, how can she say that?*
And then to think *maybe she has a point*

She seems so certain
and she's been here such a long time
Forty-one years, and change

> "Anatomy Scan" takes its title from the medical imaging procedure I had done late in my pregnancy with my daughter, which scanned all her body parts to check on their development. I liked the idea of imagining that such a scan could reveal, in visible form, the complicated emotions of marriage with children. To write it, I used an Italian poetic form, a Petrarchean sonnet.

Anatomy Scan

Cloaca of love's pain, guilt, viscous rage
Desire cramped and aching, churning bile
Resentment filling space that held our child
Intestines washed in sorrow. In these days
Of worse poor sickness, tendons strain–
Torque fibers of connection, tightened till
Striations groove the bones, recording signs
Of all they've held and borne. Yet, in the veins
Float molecules of dormant tenderness
Of longing marrow-deep. Branched dendrites reach
Grasp fragments of old laughter. Ventricles
Beat open/shut, uncertain, as I breathe
A prayer for plasmic grace to flood my cells
And lead my body not to part, but cleave.

> *This poem was inspired by looking at poignant images of lost children's toys created by the artist Ellen Fisher (see http://ellen-fisher.com), as well as by my own experience of hugging my daughter, at bedtime, after a day of cupcake-eating.*

Hannah

icing in her hair
makes my breath ache with terror
of life without her

I have always loved visiting historical sites and imagining, while I am there, that I could go travel back in time to experience what they used to be like. Spectacle Island has many layers of history, having been home to a Native American settlement, a tuberculosis hospital, a glue factory, a garbage dump that caught fire and burned for years, and finally, a dumping ground for earth excavated during Boston's Big Dig, which moved the city's highways underground. Visiting with my family, I felt many ghosts.

Ghost Crowd at the Visitors' Center
Spectacle Island, Boston Harbor

horses
manes flowing, galloping hooves
sweat snort whinny bray
here, after lives of work
they were rendered
limb from sinew
hair and skin
in vats and steam
distilled to liquids, white
sent back to bind and cleanse
the city

patients
thin gowns
over bones

MATERFAMILIAS

specks of blood
sailing on feverbeds
as they did across the bay
dreaming
of child mother friend
left safe behind

fires
burning a decade
methane fuel of our refuse
our swollen waste
smoldering to air
and leaching to sea
while land-streets shine
each morning clean

dirt
solacing, burying
barge after barge
mounting as
travelers breathe, fly
through tunnels of green-covered
speed

watching all
just a few
hunters
people of the first light

extinguished
by our beacon on a hill

grass smooths the drumlin
where my kids run
pigtails flip flops
come on let's go mom
it's so boring

ferry's wake
churns my reflection
on what you see and
what you don't
and on the island
no man is

> *Psychoanalysis has been for me a powerful path to both emotional healing and spiritual exploration, and I wish it were more widely understood. In 2003, I was happy to contribute to the field's literature by allowing my analyst at the time, Jill Comins, to write about me as an analysand she called Laura in a major journal, Psychoanalytic Dialogues. Although I did not know it then, the journal issue in which Jill's article appeared was dedicated to the memory of Emmanuel Ghent, a widely loved psychoanalyst who had recently died, and whose work, when I discovered it many years later, seemed to speak directly to me. This poem takes its title from one of his best-known essays.*

Credo
for Manny Ghent

I believe
That love hurts
That it can't always be repaired
That things, seen from many viewpoints
Are bad and trending worse—
I don't have to tell you.

I believe in surrender
To what undeniably *is*
It's fighting facts that kills you
Pain that's pure can open us

And I believe in hidden splendor
That we are spirit, huge
I have faith in resurrection
In worlds within, beyond this world

Life's a tangle to unravel
Shifts of vision can surprise
When we're wrapped in heart-and-thought-cords
With another, who can help

Trace the patterns in our chaos
Find the secrets in our dreams
Throw us a blanket, maybe, even
When we didn't even know
We were cold

"Living Water," a Petrarchean sonnet, follows in the Jewish tradition of midrash, which expands on a moment in Scripture. I was taken with the idea that the Samaritan woman may have been a prostitute or some other type of woman considered disreputable in her society, and that Jesus let himself be seen with her publicly to make the point that she and others like her are worthy of respect. I also loved the idea of her reflecting in old age and telling someone (maybe her granddaughter?) about her personal encounter with the man who came to be venerated as the son of God.

Living Water

He came to a town in Samaria, where Jacob's well was. Tired as he was from the journey, he sat down by the well. And a Samaritan woman came to draw water.

John 4

If I were married, how could I be here
alone? I said. His black eyes shone. He rose
and laid his workman's hand upon the stone.
A drink, he asked. I held the cup so near
his lips I felt their heat. He said, men fear
the water that could satisfy their souls.
Do you? I watched the warm wind blow his robe
against his skin. I said, I've ears to hear.
Just then the others came, and though he smiled
to see his men, he did not turn from me—
stood with me, woman-stranger, in the sun.

There were a thousand like him in those days,
all swearing with great passion, "I am he;"
But in my memory, he's the only one

> "Week of Wonders" evokes the feelings I had during the years when I would travel weekly for work from Boston to New York, along Amtrak's coastal route. I'd always feel a sadness leaving home in the early morning, before my children woke; but in Manhattan, I'd stay in the Wolcott Hotel, a wonderful 1904 landmark, where I imagined I felt the spirits of the people who stayed there when it was new. The poem uses the Malaysian pantoum form, in which lines repeat in a set pattern.

Week of Wonders

At bedtime, said my son, I wonder why
There's language with its crowds and crowds of words
What happens when we die and what are we
In song-soft warmth we watched the moon grow gold

There's language with its crowds and crowds of words
But orchids paired with driftwood lance the heart
In song-soft warmth we watched the moon grow gold
Like warehouse rooftops glazed with morning cloud

As orchids paired with driftwood lance the heart
My small boy asked me how'd the Big Bang start
Past warehouse rooftops' glazed with morning cloud
My coast train sails. What's gathered, scatters far

My small boy asked me how'd the Big Bang start
The hotel's spirits lounge around my room
All coast trains sail. What's gathered, scatters far
Wainscoting hides a marbled ballroom's gleam

The hotel's spirits lounge around my room
Its doll inventors, bankrupt millionaires
Wainscoting hides a marbled ballroom's gleam
The fireworks scion, racetrack king are gone

Did doll inventors, bankrupt millionaires
Watch dustlight dancing in a beam of sun?
The fireworks scion, racetrack king are gone
I see the dark and I just want and want

Watch dustlight dancing in a beam of sun
What happens what we die and what are we?
I see the dark and I just want and want
At bedtime, said my son, I wonder why

Acknowledgements

Deepest thanks are due to Mark Evan Chimsky, the first reader for all these poems, the editor of this collection, and my dear friend.

Grateful acknowledgement is also made to the editors of the publications in which the following poems first appeared:

Boston Poetry Magazine ("Anatomy Scan," "C-nsor-d," "Mother and Child," "Saving Grace," "Swimming with Dolphins")
Corium ("The Glassine Lizard")
Kind Over Matter ("Kevin Knows Color," "Materfamilias," "On Wandering," "Site-Specific," "Tonglen for Rin Norris")
Rattle ("Entanglement")
Wild Violet ("Rosary")

Copyright 2018 Kimberly Gladman Jackson
Published by Tandeta Books
Cover image: Mark Evan Chimsky
Author photo: Philip M. Jackson
Cover design: Jennie Weyman
Copyeditor: Julia Bleck

Made in the USA
Columbia, SC
10 September 2018